D0570481

PRAISE FOR WIN/WIN NETWORKING

Praise for Teresa Thomas and *Win/Win Networking: Your Guidebook for Confident and Effective Connections*

"Teresa knows that most people would rather get a tooth pulled than network. They are afraid of it, don't know what to do, and feel worried they will make a mistake. The excuses are endless! And yet, networking and connecting with other like-minded people is one of the fastest ways to grow your business and sales. Buy her book, READ the whole thing and you'll feel lighter, hopeful, and ready to see networking as the GIFT it really is."

-KIM DUKE, International Sales Coach For Women In Business

"I highly recommend this book to everyone. It has applicability to so many vocations, and even to our personal lives. I have been acting on Teresa's advice and insights in my writing career quite recently and am really pleased with where things are heading. Like Teresa herself, this book is a treasure!"

-ELLIOTT FOSTER, Author and General Counsel

"The best actionable tips I've seen from this kind of book. If you haven't picked up a copy yet, I highly recommend it."

-JEAN HANSON, Authorized Duct Tape Sales Consultant

"I love how the tips are organized in a way that are easy to find and understand. I get tired of 'how-to' books that are all fluff. This guidebook gets right to the point. I've learned so much that I'm already putting to use."

-AMY LOKKEN, Owner of MüD Modular

"Win/Win Networking really helps students get comfortable with networking and prepare for their job search. And our alumni have found it useful, too."

-LYNNE SCHUMAN, Director of Career Services

"Teresa's networking advice has given me the tools to be a better speaker and to feel more confident whether it's with a VIP or in front of a large audience. Implementing her advice even led to an invitation to be featured as a presenter at an out-of-state conference. I am always so impressed with how well she writes, speaks, and connects with her audience."

-DEREK MANESS, Director of Graduate School Outreach and Recruitment

"After just two days of picking up Win/Win Networking, I headed out to a networking event with new tips and tools to implement. The results were amazing! I used ideas from the following up section, and I am happy to announce that I had a 100% follow-up rate!"

-M. SHANNON HERNANDEZ, The Writing Whisperer

Win/Win Networking

YOUR GUIDEBOOK FOR CONFIDENT AND EFFECTIVE CONNECTIONS

Teresa Thomas

MINNEAPOLIS, MN

Copyright © 2016 by Teresa Thomas.

All rights reserved. No part of this publication may be reproduced, distributed or transmitted in any form or by any means, including photocopying, recording, or other electronic or mechanical methods, without the prior written permission of the publisher, except in the case of brief quotations embodied in critical reviews and certain other noncommercial uses permitted by copyright law.

When using quotes, please attribute them to: Teresa Thomas, www.teresa-thomas.com

Interior Book Design and Chapter Illustrations by Grace Black

Author photos by Laine Torres Photography

Cover design by Elena Dodevska

Win/Win Networking: Your Guidebook for Confident and Effective Connections. / Teresa Thomas. —2nd ed.

WinWinNetworking.com

ISBN 13: 978-1-63489-008-3

eISBN 13: 978-1-63489-009-0

Contents

With Gratitude

This guidebook is the direct result of my wonderful network which I hold in high regard. I am grateful for all of the support and encouragement I have received on this project and throughout my life and career. Above all, thank you for the ways you connect. The world becomes a better place when we treat each other well. We are all connected.

A Letter From Teresa

Confession:

I'm a professional networker. I meet and introduce people for a living. But I wasn't always this way.

As a child I was quite reserved. My teachers indicated that I was shy, observant, empathic, and diligent. And guess what—although I've since developed into a professional networker and the director of a thriving networking group, I still get nervous and shy—especially if I'm in a new environment. I created this guidebook in order to share with you how I've graduated from shy to shining when it comes to networking.

Each one of those qualities my teachers commented on (including the shyness) have helped me to become the networker I am today.

Allow me to explain:

Shy & Reserved

People who feel shy have this going for them: They are often the best listeners. Everyone wants to be truly heard, so someone who really listens stands out. A good listener also responds most appropriately in conversation because they pay attention to what others are saying instead of focusing on their own thoughts.

Observant

By observing how others make networking look so easy (or any other skill for that matter), you can glean insights into what tools and techniques are being put to use that you can try out or modify for yourself. By being observant, you also learn more about the world around you and how you can integrate into it effectively.

Empathic

The best way to feel at ease is to get out of your own head. Think about what the other person feels or needs and how you can help. As soon as you shift from a mentality of "it's all about me" to "how can I help them?" you'll feel more confident and be more effective in the ways you relate to others. I think you'll also find that your connections feel more meaningful when you practice empathy.

Diligent

To get good at and confident in anything, you need to get out there and practice. Practicing inevitably leads to making mistakes. Allowing yourself the grace to be okay with making mistakes, as well as having a sense of humor and learning from them makes you human and all the more approachable. I cannot count how many times I have made a networking faux pas. But each time, I brush myself off, learn, and improve so that I can become more confident and effective.

Now that you know my little secret, I hope you feel reassured that networking is a skill you can learn and develop with practice. I went from someone who would try to blend into the woodwork, praying to go unnoticed, to a person who finds meeting new people highly rewarding, meaningful, educational, and supportive.

Who is this for?

I've written this guide for anyone who is interested in growing and helping others grow through networking.

Since I run a women's networking group, I often resort to "she" and "her". You may also notice that I often speak to entrepreneurs and small business owners like myself. But my hope is for this networking guide to be useful to all, even if you're not a female entrepreneur. Perhaps you're a recent graduate in job-search mode, a staff member at a nonprofit, a corporate employee, an executive, or in another arena entirely. I can say with confidence that all will benefit from these insights.

This is the second edition of this guide and I view it as a body of work that will continue to grow, alongside my professional experiences and understanding. So much of what I learn about business and networking comes from connections, both new and old, for which I am thankful. If you have your own tips you would like to add, or a request to include other professions and industries, by all means share them! Everything I learn helps me to be a better resource for others, helping to boost their confidence and effectiveness in connecting with each other.

Happy Connecting!

Teresa Thomas, WIN Director
and "The Win/Win Networker"

CHAPTER ONE

What is Networking?

When I was 18 years old, my family's house burned down. No one was grievously harmed, but everything that my family owned was suddenly gone. Losing my clothing, photographs, and other belongings was deeply upsetting, but it allowed me to learn something very important: life isn't about stuff—it's about the connections we make and how we treat each other. By fostering these connections, we add meaning to our lives and lift each other up. In its essence, networking is the creation of win-win relationships which benefit everyone involved. We give and take in order to add meaning to our lives and create something bigger than ourselves. If you arrive ready to give, you will be lifted up by the generosity of others. We share our knowledge, connections, emotional support and more with each other.

During the ten-plus years I've spent organizing more than 500 networking events and workshops to help people connect, I've learned a lot about networking. My hope as a professional network nurturer is that everyone finds ways to more confidently connect with others and ask for what they need, whether it's personally or professionally.

It's up to you to ask for what you want and communicate what you do. Whether you're a student or recent graduate preparing for your career, in job transition, starting or running a business, or working for a company, networking helps you to make connections and receive ideas and inspiration to help you on your path. My goal for you is to feel more confident in making and nurturing connections and for you to leave each interaction feeling energized and motivated for what's ahead of you.

Many people participate in networking to be inspired and learn from the other participants. Some of them are looking to get back into the workforce or make a career change. Some are working as entrepreneurs or working remotely for a larger company and seek more interpersonal connections. Often, people will network as a way to gain referrals that lead to more sales or clients. Many networkers are business owners or leaders looking to increase their connections and visibility while staying in touch with other businesses, learning and keeping abreast of what's new in their industry.

Through networking and being a helpful resource, relationships are developed. By asking for what you need, others are able see how they can help. The clearer you are in your request, the easier it is for others to identify specific ways they can be of support.

A stronger network makes you a better resource.

"When you attend an event, you may not always meet people who relate to your business, but these new connections may be perfect for your clients, friends, and family. Introducing the people you meet networking to your preexisting network makes you a more valuable resource to your clients and colleagues."

—Tara Truax, marketing expert, speaker, and author

Authenticity in Networking

I also believe in being authentic about your needs. If you're looking to learn something new or need guidance about where to start, put that out there. Too often, we feel like we have to present ourselves to everyone as having it all together and knowing all the answers. Real relationships, even in business, are about meeting each other where we actually are. This means that in order to be a great networker, you have to understand your own strengths and goals.

For better connections, be yourself.

"When you network, take down the façade and bring out your best self. Personality makes us unique, interesting individuals and helps us to find the people we most want to know. Don't create a square box version of yourself. Be your own real, quirky self."

—Kelly Pratt, creative catalyst and arts administrator

CHAPTER TWO

Preparing to Network

We may not all be born as a confident, outgoing person who feels constantly at ease in a crowd. I certainly wasn't! But I began observing these people—trying to understand what made them seem so comfortable and welcoming. I realized that the source of their positive aura was their ability to draw out and lift up others around them. Although my focus was on them, what made them seem so magnetic was their attention on others.

As the Director of WIN, I've learned that even outgoing people get nervous about networking. No matter what your social disposition, there are skills and techniques you can use to be more effective, make networking feel easier, and enjoy yourself. Before you know it, this way of interacting will become second nature.

Have a Goal in Mind

Unfortunately, it's all too easy to approach networking without a clear direction. However, having professional and personal goals will make you clearer in your introductions and help you to make the most of the opportunities at hand. A goal keeps you anchored, but it should not preclude you from allowing other things to come up in your conversations. Remember that people should not be viewed simply as potential sales or job prospects, but as individuals whom you can provide and find support and who can add value to your life in many ways.

Gain and give support and accountability

"Networking can help you to be accountable to your goals and to gain support along the way. By networking, you're choosing to work on your own personal development and get out of your comfort zone. In doing so, you're rewarded by discovering people who can be a mutual source of support for your goals."

—Mary Muroski, business strategist and speaker

Determine your reasons for networking by answering the following questions:

What is one of your most important personal goals?

Example: Incorporate more travel into my life to experience various cultures and to feel more connected and adventurous by building friendships throughout the world.

What is one of your most important professional goals?

Example: To become known as the "go to" resource for my profession and the first person people think of when they seek networking expertise for information, presentations, and events.

How can networking help you to reach your goals?

Check all that apply:

- ☐ Leads to work
- ☐ Leads to business (new clients, sales)
- ☐ Strengthen connections with existing clients and referral sources
- ☐ Feel less isolated in my work, more connected
- ☐ Learn, discover, gain insights, information
- ☐ Mentor or be mentored
- ☐ Stay in tune with the market
- ☐ Keep abreast of innovations and opportunities
- ☐ Make a difference, fulfill a sense of purpose
- ☐ Re-energize or inspire myself for my work
- ☐ Gather resources to move forward
- ☐ Allow myself to be seen as a resource
- ☐ Become a better resource (the broader my network, the more it helps my clients or company)
- ☐ Increase visibility for me, my division, or company
- ☐ Build the company and/or product brand
- ☐ Meet others for collaboration or cross-support
- ☐ Other:

Become a resource to yourself

A lot of the questions you have now are the same questions that other people have when they're in your position. Document the questions that you have now so you can answer them as you continue to progress and learn. Eventually you may become an authority. This helps you to become a more valuable expert resource for others.

Make your Networking Action Plan

Keeping your networking goals in mind, what types of groups or experiences will most help you to meet your unique goals? Check all that apply:

- ☐ Professional associations
- ☐ Informative workshops/trainings
- ☐ Informal networking
- ☐ Structured networking
- ☐ Online networking/social media
- ☐ Special interest groups
- ☐ Mastermind groups
- ☐ Socially-oriented groups
- ☐ Volunteering
- ☐ Involvement in special projects
- ☐ 1:1 informational interviews or meetings
- ☐ Other:

Grow your network through professional development.

So many people put the cart before the horse when it comes to attending great events. They focus on meeting people in order to get business, ignoring the professional development and the opportunity to learn. When you attend an event with a focus on learning new ways to succeed, you may just find that without even trying to, you walk away with connections to other business owners, many who want to do business with you, thanks to your magnetic engagement.

—Steve Heap, audio, web and graphic designer

Discover the Main Points for Your Introduction

Think about the one to three main points you want to share with the people you meet at each event.

Picture it this way: If the other person were to remember only a couple of things about you, what would you want those things to be? Be sure that at least one of the points encompasses your goal. Consider having one of the key points be a call to action focused on your goal, such as an invitation to an event, your newsletter list, to sample your product or service, a request for the type of introduction or a referral you're seeking. You may also want to prepare what you want others to share with you.

These main points will change over time and in various circumstances. Before an event, often simply on the drive over, I will think about what types of attendees will be drawn to the event and what parts of my work are most important for me to share with that group. I'll share some examples from how I select my key points:

- If I'll be at a mixed-gender event, I probably won't share much about my women's networking group, but instead I'll mention how much I enjoy giving presentations to help people be more confident and effective in their networking. When I follow up, I'll include a link to my speaker website along with a brief description to make it easy for them to share groups that would find it to be of benefit.
- If I have a conference coming up, I may share what most excites me about the keynote or breakout sessions. I'll

bring promotional fliers for those who are interested in learning more and let them know about the early registration rate.

- If I'll be meeting decision makers for businesses that want to connect with more women through their marketing, I will focus on how WIN offers a variety of advertising opportunities to reach entrepreneurial women, and I will provide the contact information for our advertising sales and support.

In each of the above scenarios, my goal will be to learn more about them so I can provide the most relevant and useful information both in our conversation and when I follow up with them.

Practice for different situations.

Practice your introduction on your own and with people you meet so that you get comfortable introducing yourself. Vary it and keep it conversational (people tune out robotic introductions!). Speed networking is a good way to get comfortable with your introduction because you get a chance to repeat your introduction with a lot of people in a short time.

Connect doing what you enjoy.

"Networking happens most easily when we do things we enjoy or want to learn. People with similar interests are drawn to the event, activity, or class and it's much easier to strike up a conversation and get to know each other."
-Ann Young, sign company owner

Opportunity Evaluation Tool

Ask yourself	Assessment	How much does this matter to me?
Are the participants a fit for the type of people I'd like to meet?	□ Yes □ Not Sure □ No	□ A lot □ Somewhat □ Not much
Am I interested in the format or topic?	□ Yes □ Not Sure □ No	□ A lot □ Somewhat □ Not much
Does it fit my schedule?	□ Yes □ It's doable. □ No	□ A lot □ Somewhat □ Not much
Will this energize me or deplete my energy?	□ I will be energized □ Worth the energy □ Not worth it	□ A lot □ Somewhat □ Not much
Does it work with my budget?	□ Yes □ A stretch, but worth it □ No	□ A lot □ Somewhat □ Not much
Will this help make me a better resource to my network, clients, or team?"	□ Yes □ Not Sure □ No	□ A lot □ Somewhat □ Not much
Will I learn something useful?	□ Yes □ Not Sure □ No	□ A lot □ Somewhat □ Not much
Does this fit my professional development plan?	□ Yes □ Not Sure □ No	□ A lot □ Somewhat □ Not much
Do people whose opinion I respect attend or recommend it?	□ Yes □ Not Sure □ No	□ A lot □ Somewhat □ Not much
Other criteria you may have:	□ Yes □ Not Sure □ No	□ A lot □ Somewhat □ Not much
After considering the above, am I interested in attending?	□ Yes □ I'll give it a shot □ Not this time	

Find the group that best fits.

Take the time to find the groups that are the best fit for you and your networking goals. Check out a lot of different ones to find out where you connect. You should feel good about being a part of your group. Consider if this is a place where you will find mutual support. Find the people you can be real with. After all, you'll be spending a lot of time there.

The Opportunity Evaluation Tool gives you questions to ask yourself when you are considering networking opportunities. Use it to help you filter which are a fit for your goals.

Network with people who know your potential clients.

Another way to determine good places for you to network is to seek out places where you can connect with people who already know your clients before you do. For example, if you serve busy moms trying to balance family and a full-time job, network with other businesses that serve the same demographic. Connect with them on social media, go to conferences and events on subjects targeted to those businesses, and also visit places that directly serve your demographic. For businesses that serve the same market with which you have synergy, explore becoming strategic referral sources for each other.

Have a role.

Volunteer at networking events to curb nervousness and create an easy way to mingle. Having a role (such as helping with check-in) makes it easier to initiate conversations and see who is in attendance whom you'd like to meet. It also aids you as you exit conversations, saying something along the lines of

"I need to check on my ______. It was nice to meet you!"
xyz responsibility

My secret? Even when I don't have a role, I act as if I'm a "goodwill ambassador" by helping to make sure that each person I meet and the hosts have a good experience. For instance, introducing people to each other, being a welcoming and attentive listener, and sharing information or resources I think would be of interest.

Having an exhibit table helps break the ice.

"As an introvert, I've found that having a purpose such as a tradeshow booth at an event helps me to connect with people. It gives me a concrete reason to talk with the visitors to my table about my service, products, and how I can help them."
—Elizabeth Hagen, professional speaker and author

Create a networking kit.

A kit makes preparing for an event a no-brainer. Include things like business cards, a business card holder, nice pen, mints, small sticky notes for when you can't write on someone's business card and (of course) this networking guide/journal to help you compile your notes!

Stay organized.

Store your business cards in an easy-to-access place to avoid fumbling (e.g. jacket pocket, pocket at top or the side of purse). Get into the habit of putting your cards in the same place (just like you do your house keys) so you don't have to remember where you put them. Pack extras in your purse, laptop bag,

Networking Kit

Item	Notes
□ Business cards	Keep cards at the ready (in jacket pocket or accessible part of purse).
□ Business card holder	If you don't already have a business card holder you love and that fits your personal brand, it is a very small investment to make a great impression.
□ Extra business cards	Bring more than you think you'll need. Keep a stash of extras in your car. If you're out of cards, order some right away (many printing companies provide 24-hour turn around). If you're still working out the design, place a small order so that you'll at least have something to share.
□ Pen	Check that it works. Preferably an attractive one. Keep it at the ready, not buried in bag.
□ Directions	Print these out and double-check them ahead of time. You don't want to arrive feeling flustered from getting lost on the way to an event.
□ Mini sticky notes	To keep track of follow-up items for each person you meet, apply a sticky note to the back of their business card. These work well for glossy cards or ones that are printed on both sides.
□ Gum, mints	Enjoy this on the way to the meeting so that you'll have fresh breath when you arrive. Be sure to dispose of gum before entering the event.
□ Small envelope	Write the name of the event on a small envelope and put all of the business cards you receive into it. This makes it easier to remember where you received cards.
□ Mirror check	Are your teeth clean? Is your hair and makeup fresh? Wear something that's professional and makes you feel confident and look great. Bonus if it includes a jacket with pockets that makes it easier to have your business cards and a pen available.
□ Know your goal(s)	Know in advance your goals for attending the event so that you're clear in the way you introduce yourself and the information you share.
□ Arrive early	It's much easier to network when you're one of the first to arrive because you're helping to set the scene. If you arrive early, ask the host if you can help in any way.
□	
□	
□	

glove compartment, or briefcase so when you run out or go to an impromptu networking event, you will always have some on hand.

Use the envelope method for organizing business cards.

Keep a stack of small envelopes next to your business cards, and bring one to each networking event you attend. Note the event and date on the outside of the envelope and include a note for the date when you will follow up. Put all of the cards you collect during your event in the envelope.

When you're ready to follow up, you'll remember where you met each person. After you've followed up, you can either toss the contents or tuck the envelope with the details written on it into a shoebox with others.

Dress in a way that makes you feel confident

This isn't the time to wear the pants that might be too tight or the shirt that just doesn't feel like it fits your personality. The more confident and relaxed you are, the more you will attract others to you and the more self-assured you will be in approaching people and starting up conversations. Wear a professional outfit that makes you feel confident and look great.

Let the mirror reflect your best self.

"Your professional image reflects how you feel about yourself and how you want the world to feel about you. You are a walking advertisement for the world to see."

-Laura Madden, stylist, model, and confidence coach

CHAPTER THREE

Networking In Action

By building your network, you're crafting a support system as well as establishing a group of people who, by getting to know you and developing trust, end up serving as your best, most authentic salesforce. The credibility of someone else talking about you is much higher than simply tooting your own horn. Your goal should be to learn as much as possible about these new connections so that you, in turn, are able to share useful or interesting information.

The fastest way to put others and yourself at ease is to give undivided attention to the person with whom you're speaking. This will calm your nerves by paying attention to someone else instead of worrying about yourself. It also makes you more memorable and makes people want to know you.

Even if you don't have much time for your own introduction, be sure you get the other person's contact information. The person will be more likely to call and work with you if they consider you a potential asset. Shift to showing interest instead of trying to be interesting.

Place your nametag smartly.

Wear your name tag just a few inches down and on your right side (near your right collarbone). That is where people's eyes are naturally drawn when you shake hands.

Don't wear your nametag so far down that it is placed somewhere uncomfortable for others to look. If you are provided with a nametag on a lanyard that hangs around your neck, consider knotting the back to bring it higher than navel level.

If you have long hair, pull it back and over your shoulder so that your nametag is visible.

If the event has you fill out your own nametag, I suggest including both your first and last name along with the name of your business or the profession you hold or are seeking.

If you are wearing a jacket, sweater, or scarf, make sure that the nametag is not covered up by it.

If you frequently network, consider getting a professional nametag made with your full name and business. To really have your badge stand out, you can include your logo along with the font and color of your brand. The badge I use is magnetic so I don't have to worry about it damaging my clothes or falling off. So that you don't forget it, keep it in a side pocket of your bag or purse or in your glove compartment. (Magnetic badges cannot be worn by those with pacemakers. They need to be stored away from credit cards or cards that have a scanning strip on the back.)

Lead with an authentic introduction.

My preference is for an introduction that sounds more conversational than recited. There are so many "how-tos" about how to create an introduction and you may have a favorite already. This is my tried-and-true formula for introductions:

- Focus on results you provide (not your title)
- Have a goal in mind for your introduction and share between one and three key things you want people to know about you.
- Don't stress about getting it perfect—only you know the key points you wish to share.
- Remain authentic. Adjust your introduction according to the circumstances and the people you meet.
- If possible, ask the other person about themselves first. That way you will have a better sense of the information you can share that will be most relevant to them.

Here is an example of how I often introduce myself using this formula:

"I'm a Connector. I'm constantly thinking about "who needs to know who" and about what resources they'll find useful. I get to do that through running a group called Women In Networking and by giving presentations to help people to be more confident and effective in their networking." Any other key points I share are determined by who I am meeting and what my main goal is for that particular event (see the previous section in this guidebook, Discover your main points for your introduction).

Take two steps.

Making connections during networking is a two-step process:

1. Learn about them.
2. Let them learn about you.

Get out of your own head and be fully present. Listen to your conversational partner and express genuine interest in that person. Relationship building is about building trust. People want to know you, like you, and trust you before they ever refer you to others, become your client, or even future employer.

Introduce yourself with confidence. By keeping your introduction focused on key points and what most excites you about your profession (don't get long-winded about every single thing you do!) they will usually want to know more. When they're asking questions, it means they're truly engaged and learning and you'll have a better sense of whether they are potentially interested in doing business with you.

Asking about what they need and how you could help each other is another great way to get to know each other and build the trust that leads to referrals.

Don't isolate yourself from opportunities.

"Do great opportunities fall in your lap? No! They usually come from the people you know and meet."
—Kristi Hemmer, empowerment coach

Keep your body language at ease.

This helps you to be approachable. Smile, make eye contact, have an open and confident posture and avoid crossing your arms. Instead of standing squared off with another person, stand in a slight "V" to create an opening for other people to easily join in your conversation.

If you aren't sure what to do with your hands, you will appear more inviting to others if you have them behind your back or if you have your arms down and in front of you with your fingers lightly holding each other.

Holding an open and confident posture might feel awkward at first but with practice, it becomes natural. The bonus is that confident body language makes you feel more confident even when you're nervous.

In my presentations, I refer to standing in a slight "V" as creating a "networking vortex" that helps to attract and invite other people into your conversation. I demonstrate how easy it is to encourage a passer-by to join in a conversation by holding out an arm and saying, "Come join our conversation!" (I call it the "swoop that saves the day" because it helps everyone involved with entering and exiting conversations.)

Overcome networking jitters.

I've found that these tips help immensely when you're nervous about networking:

1. Seek out the positive-looking people (those with open body language and a friendly expression) in the room.

2. Focus on making it a valuable and engaging experience for others instead of worrying and obsessing about you.

3. Find out what the person you're meeting needs so that when you share information, it's relevant and helpful. When you put others in the spotlight and help them to shine, it reflects back onto you!

4. Take a deep breath and remember you're in good company. Other people are nervous, too. If you can help them out, they will be relieved and eager to know more about you. It's as simple as offering to hold a glass while someone reaches for their business cards or introducing people to one another.

Bonus tip:

On the drive over, listen to the type of music or podcast that helps you to feel strong and confident. Some professional speakers listen to a "power song" before they go on stage. You can do that, too!

Seek out and be the positive.

"Approach people with a nice positive energy. Look for signals that you are dealing with what I call Adders (the positive, helpful people). Know that they likely have something about them that you could benefit from and that they could benefit from meeting you, too. When you come across a Subtractor (clue: they complain about everything), just say "Nice to meet you" and step away. "

—Dr Verna Price, Power of People expert and author

Network in pairs.

I like to call this "**collaborative networking**." Network in conjunction with your friends, colleagues and best clients. Find out where your favorite clients like to network and go with them. There are several benefits to this system:

1. A "wing person" allows you to cover much more ground.
2. You'll be able to lift each other up as you meet new people. It's much easier to compliment someone else than to constantly sell your own services, and it also conveys that you are a person who is supportive and willing to help others.
3. Rather than staying joined at the hip, use each other as a home-base. Venture off to meet people and when it makes sense, introduce the people you meet to your friend. Bonus: This makes it much easier to gracefully enter and exit conversations!
4. If you are at a seated event, sit at different tables or across the table from each other. That way, you will each get to know the people to the right and left of you while feeling more secure that your friend isn't far away.
5. By attending events with your best clients, you'll meet people similar to your ideal client who then can lead to great referrals or even become clients themselves.

Use familiar language.

Unless you are amongst colleagues who are used to a specific way of conversing, use language that is commonly understood. Be wary of industry-speak, slang, technical terminology, insider language, acronyms, and other diction that will distance you from others. If you talk above someone's head, they're likely to tune out.

Connect others.

Introduce people to each other, and encourage friendly people walking by at a networking event to join your conversation. You'll stand out by helping them to network with each other, and they will be intrigued to learn more about you.

Be open to new connections.

"Open yourself up to new connections, and you're sure to find people who you can learn from, who want to learn from you, and who want to be your clients and collaborate with you. There are people out there who are going to contribute to your success, learning, inspiration, and future projects."
—Loren Lockman, wellness center owner

Don't be overly generous with your business cards.

Don't give out more than one business card or piece of marketing material unless someone specifically asks for it. Otherwise, it's just annoying and wasteful (the extras will likely just get tossed right away). With so much information available online, the people you meet are not likely to hold onto your card for very long, preferring to visit your website or connect on social media to keep in touch.

Tips for remembering names.

The key here is to be fully present. It's easy to get nervous and caught up in our own heads about how we will introduce ourselves (so much so that we don't even hear what the other person says). Give the other person your full attention for their introduction. When you introduce yourself, state your own name clearly. Not rushing through your name will help them to remember your name.

If they are wearing a nametag, looking at their name helps to create a visual imprint to strengthen memory. I like to repeat their name so that I have another auditory imprint. For example, "It's nice to meet you, Mary!"

Other experts share tips to use name/word association. For example, if someone met me they might remember my name (Teresa Thomas) by picturing a tree with a saw along with someone they know who has the name Thomas. I personally find it distracting because in the time I'm trying to come up with name associations, I may have missed the other things they shared in their introduction. Sometimes I will use name/word association but not while they are introducing themselves to me (e.g. if I'm looking at a name in a program or check-in list).

What to do when you've forgotten a name or face.

I meet so many people each week that this is a problem I face regularly. Sometimes, I'll even forget the name of a good friend because so many names are fighting for space in my mind. And oftentimes, I won't recall the face of someone I've met several times before. On the other hand, sometimes I remember an uncanny amount of details about someone I only met briefly many years ago. I'm not sure how the human mind works, but I have found some useful tools.

Perhaps you can't remember if you've met someone before, or think you have met but you can't remember the details. In order to not reveal your memory lapse, avoid launching into an introduction until you're sure it's the first time you've met. If they look familiar, say something like, "You look so familiar. I meet a lot of people in my work. Do you know if we've met?" Otherwise, you can keep your greeting general, asking something like, "How did you find out about this event?" or "How are you connected with the host?" They're likely to lead off from there with an introduction or an indication that you have already met.

If it's still unclear and you haven't found an opportunity to learn their name, you can offer yours first, saying "I'm so-and-so." If they say, "Yes, we've met," you can respond, "I'm terrible with remembering names so I like to share mine in case the other person doesn't remember. Speaking of which, could you remind me of your name?" This takes the pressure off of them and saves you from some of the embarrassment of admitting you can't remember if you've met.

Learn some essential exit strategies.

Just as important as a graceful entrance is a graceful exit. To avoid missing out on mingling with many different groups of people, a set of proven exit strategies is essential. Here are a few of my top picks:

- Introduce a new person to the conversation. After you have introduced newcomers to each other and gotten them started in conversation, it makes it easy to excuse yourself, and they will be grateful to you for helping to make it easier for them to meet new people.

- Mention that someone you planned to talk to is nearby and excuse yourself.
- Note that you have something you need to attend to or check in on and excuse yourself. This is where volunteering or having a role in the event really helps.
- Invite the person to walk over to the food area or excuse yourself to get a refreshment.
- Ask if the person you're chatting with has met anyone at the event whom they think you should meet. If so, either ask if they'd be willing to introduce you or if they could point the person out to you. This method is great because it becomes an entrance strategy as well.
- Offer to introduce the person you're speaking with to someone you think they'd like to meet. Once you've made the introduction, you can step away.
- Simply state that you enjoyed meeting them and that you're excusing yourself so that you can both meet other great people. For those you'd like to stay connected with, ask for their card and make a goal of following up with an email or via LinkedIn later.

CHAPTER FOUR

Follow Up

Do you have a follow-up plan?

You may meet a lot of great people but having a plan for staying connected is the key for having them in your network. You've probably heard, "the fortune is in the follow up" and it's true. Relationships, business and referrals usually don't happen instantaneously. They take time to nurture and build trust.

LinkedIn, Facebook, cards, phone calls, letters, emails, a newsletter (ask for or give permission to sign up), and even a resume (when appropriate) are all great ways to stay in touch.

I advise that you suggest a resume only if your job search had been part of your conversation and if they expressed interest in receiving it. Usually, a link to your LinkedIn profile will be sufficient and is even easier for them to share if they know of someone hiring for the type of position you are seeking. Be considerate of what will work best for them.

For the top people you want to stay connected with, don't leave it at just one hit or miss follow up. Have a plan for connecting in a variety of ways over time.

Here are some easy ways you can stay connected:

- Share a useful resource you come across
- Invite them to reconnect at an event you'll be attending
- Recommend them to someone who could use their product or service
- Offer to introduce them to someone you think would be a beneficial connection
- Comment on an interesting post they make on social media.

Leverage LinkedIn

LinkedIn is an easy way to follow up and stay connected with lots of people. It takes the pressure off because you can connect on LinkedIn with someone you haven't seen for a while without feeling pushy. It's also good for staying connected with someone when you're not yet sure how exactly you can help each other.

Follow up is a process.

"When you email or call someone ONCE and they don't get back to you – don't take it personally. Listen. The reason they didn't get back to you? Let me count the ways: Their computer blew up. It hit their spam file. Their dog got sick. They are traveling. They are busy with clients. They are at a trade show. They hit some financial difficulty and are embarrassed to contact you. So quit whining and follow-up with someone today. And don't say to them "I've emailed/called you x times and you haven't gotten back to me." That's a deal killer."

—Kim Duke, international sales expert

If you're a frequent networker and worried about going over your quota for inviting others to connect, send a friendly email or note saying, "If you'd like to stay connected on LinkedIn, my profile URL is (link)."

When connecting on LinkedIn, try to avoid using the generic pre-populated message. Tailor the message to your own words including how you've met the person (e.g. noting the conference where you met them and a highlight from your conversation). A personalized message leaves a much better impression and helps you stand out. Not everyone on LinkedIn uses it regularly so don't rely on it alone to stay connected.

Recap conversations to connect

"Take your connections further by recapping a highlight when you follow up. It also helps people think of other things you can connect about in the future. When you recap what you heard someone say, it makes them feel special for being remembered."
—Amy Jauman, training and professional development consultant

Connecting to get to know someone.

Think about who you would like to get to know better, why and how you'll go about it. Write out your answers to the following questions or just think this through.

Example: *My colleague is always so motivated and excited by her work that it rubs off on everyone around her. I wonder what keeps her so interested. I'd like to get to know her better and be inspired to discover my own motivation. The next time I see her, I'll be sure to let her know how impressed I am and to ask her more about herself and how she stays so driven.*

Who are you connected with that you would like to get to know better?

Who is a good role model for you?

Who would it be good for you to be connected with to fulfill your ambitions?

Who shares your same target market but serves them in a different way? How might you help each other?

How could you go about getting to know them better? What action will you take?

Reconnecting with lapsed connections.

Although some (or a lot) of time has passed since you last connected, take a moment to think about or write down who you wish to re-connect with, and why and how you'll go about it.

Example: *My former supervisor had such lofty ambitions. I'd love to learn how he has progressed. I just read an article I think he would find useful. I will connect with him on LinkedIn and send the article. If I hear back from him, I'll offer to take him to lunch so that we can catch up more.*

Who would you like to reconnect with and why?

How could you go about reconnecting? What action will you take?

Scripts for following up.

When you follow up with someone you've met, remind them of how you met and how or why you'd like to stay connected. I've written a basic introduction and useful talking points to serve as an easy guide. Adjust the following to your own voice:

The Introduction:

Hello____________, it was so nice to meet you at __________
name *event*

The Body (mix & match):

I appreciated what you shared about____________
topic

AND/OR

How fun that we have __________ in common!
subject/person

AND/OR

It was interesting to hear about the work you do in __________
their profession/company

AND/OR

I thought about a resource that might be of interest to you:

____
article/link/organization

AND/OR

There is an upcoming event I think you'll be interested in:

________________.
name of the event

I will be attending and it would be great to see you there!

The Closing (mix & match):

I'd like to stay connected with you on LinkedIn. Here is my URL: ________________
your LinkedIn profile URL

AND/OR

If you'd like to receive updates from me, you can subscribe to my__________________ by visiting _____________
newsletter/blog *web address*

If you have a newsletter, please feel free to add me.

AND/OR

After learning about your _________________, I think we'd
work/business/target market

be good ____ for
referral sources/possible collaborators/resources

for each other.

If you'd like to explore that, let me know if

you'd like to ______________________________
meet/have a phone call/discuss more via email

Best regards,
your name

Template for requesting testimonials.

Testimonials do wonders for building a trusted reputation. But people are busy so they might not respond to an open referral request or they'll say something general that doesn't quite speak to the terrific experience they had with you.

Make it easy for people to provide referrals by summarizing what you've heard them say. Let them know how you would use their testimonial (e.g. on your website or sales material).

Adjust the following template for your own purposes:

Hello ________ ,
name

Thank you for your kind remark about the ____________
product or service

I'm so glad you were happy with your experience.

I would like to use what you wrote as a testimonial. I tried to sum up what you shared with me below:

Summarize their testimonial- their name, their business (and link if online)

Please let me know if I have your permission to use this as a testimonial or if you have any tweaks or edits you'd like to suggest.

Optional: If you'd be willing to post this to my LinkedIn profile, I'd be most appreciative.

I look forward to hearing from you. It's a pleasure doing business with you.

Best regards,

Your name

CHAPTER FIVE

Referral Savvy

It's valuable to have people in your network who are well-connected, respected and who always have good referrals to suggest. You can be that type of person to the people in your network! You will build your reputation as being a trusted "go to" source when you are able to recommend quality referrals for services and products. Here are some things to keep in mind:

Get to know people in a wide range of industries.

Keep note on the businesses that have provided you with the best service or your favorite products.

Be sure that you trust the referrals you give and know their services or products are stellar. Just because you know someone, does not mean they would be a good referral. Remember, your reputation is tied to the types of referrals you give.

If you are asked to provide a referral for a business, only share what you know directly about the person or business. For example, I have a lot of people in my network but have not personally experienced using their product or service. If I get asked about the quality of a business I haven't used myself, I would share something like, "I haven't had the chance to work with her yet but I can tell you that she is an active member, very professional and a skilled communicator. I know several people who have commented on having a wonderful experience working with her. I suggest asking her for some referrals from clients."

Likewise, it's important to understand that not everyone will be the right person to refer you to others. They need to get to know you and the experience you provide. Put your focus on gaining referrals from those who can speak directly about what you offer.

Just starting out in business? Sample your product or service to people who are supportive, well-connected and enthusiastic. Ask if you can request a testimonial if they have a good experience.

Just starting a career? Ask past employers, professors, internship or volunteer supervisors for recommendations.

Give more than you take. Be a great referral for others. That is how you become a valuable and respected resource that people want to associate with in their network.

Be a patron of your network.

"Make it a point to hire vendors and service providers who are also your clients or biggest fans. Leverage those relationships to be a win/win networker."

—Wendy Blomseth, sales executive

Build your empire.

"Create a pyramid—business empire—envisioning your network as triangle. Each level has bricks, and these are the business owners who can help you to take your business to the next level (photographers, coaches, designers, marketers). Figure out the people y need to build your business, and then look for your key players. Network to find these people to prepare to move to the next level. Work together with these people as a team to make it work."
—Lori Bestler, mind coach and motivational speaker

Be "referrable."

Provide great customer service, follow through, products or services. Develop and maintain a solid reputation. Actively network and nurture the connections you have so that you stay relevant and memorable.

Referrals List

Being a great resource for quality referrals makes you even more valuable to your network. Create a list to have on hand of top experts in your network with whom you would confidently trade referrals.

I've listed some fields to get you started.

Expertise	Contact Name	Contact Details
Accountant		
Acupuncture		
Aesthetician		
Auto Mechanic		
Bookkeeper		
Business or Career Coach		
Caterer		
Chiropractor		
Cleaning Company		
Concierge Services		
Contractor		
Copywriter		
Dentist		
Doctor		
Electrician		
Event Planner		
Financial Planner		
Graphic Designer		
Hair Stylist		

Insurance		
Interior Designer		
Landscaper		
Lawyer		
Life Coach		
Marketing Coach		
Massage Therapist		
Personal Trainer		
Photographer		
Plumber		
Professional Organizer		
Public Relations		
Realtor		
Social Media Strategist		
Tech Support		
Therapist		
Veterinarian		
Virtual Assistant		
Web Designer		

CHAPTER SIX

Finding Balance

Is it possible to over-network?

Yes. If you're finding that you don't have the time to follow up with great connections you've made or you're feeling exhausted from being in too many extroverted environments, it may be time to pace yourself. Set aside time to unwind and take action on those crucial next steps, such as connecting on LinkedIn, sending a nice email, note or invitation to a previous connection, etc. Network in a way that fuels your business and you.

I use an enormous full year wall calendar to help me make sure I'm scheduling enough down-time. I use one color of small Post-Its on the days I'll be in highly extroverted environments (e.g. speaking at or facilitating events) and another color to ensure that I schedule "refuel" time. That way, I can see at a glance when I'll be expending a lot of energy so that I can strategically schedule in time for self-care.

Set an event quota.

"Use a quota for how many networking events you'll attend so that you know you're doing enough without feeling overwhelmed. Look for "kindred spirits" instead of raking in large quantities of new contacts. Partner or surround yourself with people who balance you out so that everyone honors their own strengths and authenticity."

—From an interview by Marie Forleo with Susan Cain, author of Quiet

Value your own time.

During WIN's 2011 Conference, keynote speaker Kim Duke, the Sales Diva, advised the audience to "just say no" to too many coffee meetings. She highlighted the importance of being careful with your time, which is precious and can easily be eaten up when you're running around town. I can't believe how many times this topic has arisen among WIN members, who struggle to free up time and money without losing the chance to expand their networks.

Here are some of the best solutions I've uncovered:

1. Ask yourself whether or not the meeting is instrumental for your business. If it's obvious that it would contribute positively, such as a key partnership or bringing in revenue, then allow it to take priority.
2. Book your important projects and office-time as early as possible on your calendar so that you don't give up the time you need to spend getting work done.

3. Cluster meetings in the same part of town (or better yet at your office or close to you) so that you cut down on transportation time.
4. When connecting with someone, start with a phone meeting or have them email you the questions and details they want to discuss. If it turns out there is more you'd like to discuss, then you can decide if you want to continue the conversation by email, phone, or in person.
5. When faced with "get to know you" invitations, suggest that you meet up at one of the events you already plan to attend. This way, you can have a brief conversation with the person and you both have the chance to meet other people too.

Here are a few sample scripts you may wish to use if you would like to avoid coffee meetings:

"Thank you for the invitation. A coffee meeting won't work for me but I could do a phone call. How do either of these dates and times work for you?"

"My schedule is full but I've got an idea. Here are a few events I'll be at over the next month. If you can attend one of these, we could meet up a few minutes early and then both have a chance to meet lots of other people, too."

Schedule downtime after big events.

Whether you're introverted or extroverted, scheduling downtime will help you to re-center, reenergize, and allows you to absorb what you learned/experienced after a big event, whether a seminar, weekend networking event, wedding, or family time.

—Sarah Larson, licensed acupuncturist

CHAPTER SEVEN

Networking Journal

Use this section to document your networking activities.

Sometimes we get so busy we don't take the time to reflect on what we want to experience, what we've learned, the action steps we'd like to take, and what we would like to do differently next time. The following pages are for you to document these things. By taking the time now to think through your networking activities, you will gain clarity on where and how you wish to network to get the best results for your networking goals.

Before you head out to an event, think through the one to three key points you want to include in your introduction.

At the event, take notes on the highlights of what you learned, the actions you will take, and your top connections for follow up.

Immediately after the event, reflect on whether this is the type of event you would like to attend again. Consider what you have learned about yourself and your networking in order to have a better networking experience next time.

Event Topic: ______________________________

Presenter: ________________ Date: ____________________

Key point(s) to include when I introduce myself today:

1) ____
2) ____
3) ____

Three things I learned:

1) ____
2) ____
3) ____

Follow-up actions:

1) ____
2) ____
3) ____

Would I attend this type of event again?

☆ ☆ ☆ ☆ ☆

Why or why not?

Follow-up actions:

1) ____
2) ____
3) ____

General Notes

"Surround yourself with only people who are going to lift you higher."

— Oprah Winfrey

Event Topic: ______________________________

Presenter: ________________ Date: ____________________

Key point(s) to include when I introduce myself today:

1) ____
2) ____
3) ____

Three things I learned:

1) ____
2) ____
3) ____

Follow-up actions:

1) ____
2) ____
3) ____

Would I attend this type of event again?

☆ ☆ ☆ ☆ ☆

Why or why not?

Follow-up actions:

1) ____
2) ____
3) ____

General Notes

"The greatest gift we can give one another is rapt attention to one another's existencev."

-Sue Atchley Ebaugh

Event Topic: ______________________

Presenter: ______________ Date: ________________

Key point(s) to include when I introduce myself today:

1) ______________________________
2) ______________________________
3) ______________________________

Three things I learned:

1) ______________________________
2) ______________________________
3) ______________________________

Follow-up actions:

1) ______________________________
2) ______________________________
3) ______________________________

Would I attend this type of event again?

☆ ☆ ☆ ☆ ☆

Why or why not?

Follow-up actions:

1) ______________________________
2) ______________________________
3) ______________________________

General Notes

"Relationships are all there is. Everything in the universe only exists because it is in relationship to everything else. Nothing exists in isolation. We have to stop pretending we are individuals that can go it alone."

— Margaret J. Wheatley

Event Topic: ______________________

Presenter: ______________ Date: ______________

Key point(s) to include when I introduce myself today:

1) ______________________
2) ______________________
3) ______________________

Three things I learned:

1) ______________________
2) ______________________
3) ______________________

Follow-up actions:

1) ______________________
2) ______________________
3) ______________________

Would I attend this type of event again?

☆ ☆ ☆ ☆ ☆

Why or why not?

Follow-up actions:

1) ______________________
2) ______________________
3) ______________________

General Notes

"We have two ears and one mouth so that we can listen twice as much as we speak."

-Epictetus

Event Topic: ______________________

Presenter: ______________ Date: ________________

Key point(s) to include when I introduce myself today:

1) ____
2) ____
3) ____

Three things I learned:

1) ____
2) ____
3) ____

Follow-up actions:

1) ____
2) ____
3) ____

Would I attend this type of event again?

☆ ☆ ☆ ☆ ☆

Why or why not?

Follow-up actions:

1) ____
2) ____
3) ____

General Notes

"If you want to lift yourself up, lift up someone else."

Booker T. Washington

Event Topic: ________________________

Presenter: ________________ Date: ____________________

Key point(s) to include when I introduce myself today:

1) ____
2) ____
3) ____

Three things I learned:

1) ____
2) ____
3) ____

Follow-up actions:

1) ____
2) ____
3) ____

Would I attend this type of event again?

☆ ☆ ☆ ☆ ☆

Why or why not?

Follow-up actions:

1) ____
2) ____
3) ____

General Notes

"Treat people as if they were what they ought to be, and you help them to become what they are capable of being."
— Johann Wolfgang von Goethe

Event Topic: ____________________

Presenter: ______________ Date: ________________

Key point(s) to include when I introduce myself today:

1) ____
2) ____
3) ____

Three things I learned:

1) ____
2) ____
3) ____

Follow-up actions:

1) ____
2) ____
3) ____

Would I attend this type of event again?

☆ ☆ ☆ ☆ ☆

Why or why not?

Follow-up actions:

1) ____
2) ____
3) ____

General Notes

"Sometimes, idealistic people are put off the whole business of networking as something tainted by flattery and the pursuit of selfish advantage But virtue in obscurity is rewarded only in heaven. To succeed in this world you have to be known to people."

- Supreme Court Justice Sonia Sotomayor

Event Topic: ______________________________

Presenter: ____________________ Date: ________________________

Key point(s) to include when I introduce myself today:

1) ____
2) ____
3) ____

Three things I learned:

1) ____
2) ____
3) ____

Follow-up actions:

1) ____
2) ____
3) ____

Would I attend this type of event again?

☆ ☆ ☆ ☆ ☆

Why or why not?

Follow-up actions:

1) ____
2) ____
3) ____

General Notes

"None of us create value all by ourselves; it's our connectedness that lets us create work. We're doing stuff with other people. And these people—a network, using the more technical term—in our lives shape who we are (by influencing what we think about) and what we make (by helping us get things done). So I am pretty thoughtful about who gets on my calendar and making sure to stay in touch with those whose opinions and ideas I want to shape mine."

— Nilofer Merchant

Event Topic: ______________________________

Presenter: ____________________ Date: ________________________

Key point(s) to include when I introduce myself today:

1) ____
2) ____
3) ____

Three things I learned:

1) ____
2) ____
3) ____

Follow-up actions:

1) ____
2) ____
3) ____

Would I attend this type of event again?

☆ ☆ ☆ ☆ ☆

Why or why not?

Follow-up actions:

1) ____
2) ____
3) ____

General Notes

"My Golden Rule of Networking is simple: Don't keep score."
- Harvey Mackay

Event Topic: ______________________________

Presenter: ________________ Date: ____________________

Key point(s) to include when I introduce myself today:

1) ____
2) ____
3) ____

Three things I learned:

1) ____
2) ____
3) ____

Follow-up actions:

1) ____
2) ____
3) ____

Would I attend this type of event again?

☆ ☆ ☆ ☆ ☆

Why or why not?

Follow-up actions:

1) ____
2) ____
3) ____

General Notes

"Smart business people understand the value of networking. Put simply, expanding your contacts improves your chances to build good relationships, discover leads and generate increased sales."

— Dale Carnegie

CHAPTER EIGHT

More Networking Tips

We all have insights we can share with each other. Interspersed throughout the guidebook and in the following articles are some of my favorite networking tips as shared by wonderful people I've met through networking.

Share the spotlight.

"When you shine a light on others, it reflects back on you."
—Teresa Thomas

The Top Six Elevator Pitch Mistakes

By Amy Zastrow

An elevator pitch is a quick overview of who you are, what you do, and why the other person should care. It's called an elevator pitch because it should be given in the time it takes someone to ride an elevator (usually 30-60 seconds.) Avoid these top six elevator pitch mistakes:

1. Expecting immediate sales.

An elevator pitch is not a sales pitch! Very few pitches end in an immediate sale – especially those with higher priced products or services. One statistic states that less than 3% of the people you encounter are ready to buy. That means in a room of 100 people, only three people are ready to buy what you have to offer (and how likely are you to find them?) Therefore, you want to position yourself so other people remember you when they are ready to buy or talk to someone else who is ready to buy!

2. Trying to say too much.

There is no way you can explain all that you do in 30 or 60 seconds, so don't even try. The best thing you can do is to give an overview of what you do and generate interest so you can continue the conversation later.

3. Making it all about you.

The temptation is to tell people all about your credentials, how long you have been in business, etc. But truthfully, no one really cares. They are listening for "What's In It For Me?" (You remember that popular radio station WII-FM, don't you?). Therefore, always focus on them, their problems and how you can help them resolve them.

4. Assuming that a great pitch needs to be cute or clever.

A great elevator pitch is one that works, period. It clearly communicates what one has to offer, how it helps resolve problems and if interested, what the other person needs to do next. So don't try to be something you are not! Be yourself and communicate in a simple but straightforward way.

5. Stating that you can help "anyone."

Every person you meet has about 300 names in their brain. Your job is to help them sort through these names to identify someone you can help. Hint: it may not be the person in front of you!

6. Not making a clear request.

Most people want to help others, especially at networking events where other people are in the same boat as you (at least smart networkers do). Therefore, help them help you by making a simple but specific request.

© Amy Zastrow is The Kick Butt Business Mentor with Success Architects. LLC. For guidance on developing an elevator pitch that works for you, order her workbook, "Elevator Pitches Made Easy" from KickButtToday.com.

10 Must Have People for an A-List Professional Network

By Tai Goodwin

It is important to know the two Qs as you build out your network: quality and quantity. But have you considered the importance of having a well-rounded network?

In this job market, having a strong network is critical to your professional survival. There are plenty of tips and articles on where to find people, how and when to connect to them, and even what you need to say to attract and maintain your network. This article focuses on who should be in your network

The top 10 people that should be in your network:

1. The Mentor:

This is the person who has reached the level of success you aspire to have. You can learn from their success as well as their mistakes. Heed their wisdom and experience. This relationship offers a unique perspective because they have known you through several peaks and valleys in your life and watched you evolve.

2. The Coach:

The coach is someone who comes in at different times in your life. They help with critical decisions and transitions and offer an objective perspective with no strings attached.

3. The Industry Insider:

This is someone in your chosen field who has expert-level information or access to it. This person will keep you informed of what's happening now and what the next big thing is. Invite them to be a sounding board for your next innovative idea.

4. The Trendsetter:

This is someone outside of your chosen industry who always has the latest buzz. It can be on any topic that you find interesting. The goal in having this person in your network is to look for those connections that spark innovation via the unconventional. It will also help you keep your conversations interesting.

5. The Connector:

This is a person who has access to people, resources, and information. As soon as they come across something related to you, they are sending you an e-mail or picking up the phone. Connectors are great at uncovering unique ways to make connections, finding resources and opportunities that most people would overlook.

6. The Idealist:

This is the person in your network you can dream with. No matter how "out there" your latest idea is, this is the person who will help you brainstorm ways to make it happen. Without judgment, they are focused on helping you flesh out your dreams in high definition, even if you don't have a solid plan yet on how to make it happen.

7. The Realist:

On the flip side, you still need the person who will help you keep it real. This is the person who will give you the raised eyebrow when your expectations exceed your effort. These are not people who knock down your dreams, rather they challenge you to actively make your dream happen.

8. The Visionary:

Visionary people inspire you by their journey. They are similar to the Idealist, but the visionary can help you envision an actual plan to reach your goal. One personal encounter with this type of person can powerfully change the direction of your thinking and life.

9. The Partner:

You need to have someone who is in a similar place and on a similar path to share with. In fact, partners do a lot of sharing. This is a person you can share the wins and woes with. Partners will also share resources, opportunities, and information.

10. The Wanna-Be:

This is someone to whom you can serve as a mentor. Someone you can help shape and guide based on your experiences. One of the best ways to tell that you understand something is to be able to explain it to someone else. And sometimes, one of the best motivators for pushing through obstacles and hardship is knowing that someone is watching.

Obviously you will want to have more than 10 people in your network. The trick is to make sure you are building a diverse network by adding people from different industries, backgrounds, age groups, ethnic groups, etc. that fit into the roles listed above. Building a deep network by only including people from your current profession or business focus leaves too many stones unturned, limiting potential opportunities.

Serious about building a strong professional network that can actually provide the leverage you need to make progress at work or in your business? Evaluate your current network and get started filling in the gaps.

© Tai Goodwin, Bankable Brilliance Catalyst. Visit TaiGoodwin.com to learn how she can help you brand your own brilliance by turning what you know into information products and signature programs.

Activity: Find your 10 must-have people for an A-List professional network.

Read Tai Goodwin's article, *10 Must Have People for an A-List Professional Network* (preceding). Then use this assignment to evaluate your own A-List and start filling in the gaps. Fill in names of people that fulfill each of these categories for you.

You may have more than one name listed under a category. That's great, since you'll want to have a diverse network of people from different industries, backgrounds, age groups and cultures. If there categories for which you didn't list anyone, make a note about an action step you will take to seek that type of person out for your network.

Soon, you'll have your very own A-List!

My Mentor:
My Coach:
My Industry Insider:
My Trendsetter:
My Connector:
My Idealist:
My Realist:
My Visionary:
My Partner:
My Wannabe:

Who is on your "Most Wanted" list?

By Deb Brown

Have you ever daydreamed about people you would LOVE to work for?

It may be someone you have heard speak or a guru from whom you have learned. One way or another you know how fun it would be to have them as a client. You can add them to your "Most Wanted Client" list.

The only problem is there is a gap between the two of you Your fantasy client may not even know you are alive. How do you get them to notice you?

One technique people use is to call or email and start pushing their products or services. I can guarantee this will repel the clients you most desire to serve. I have been approached by numerous people who want me to sell their product to my clients as a great gift. While I appreciate being aware of the things that are out there, it is obvious by their approach that they are not interested in me. They are only interested in selling their stuff.

If you really want to make your dream clients become a reality, show an interest in them.

You can connect with them on social media. You can make a phone call and find out about them. You can send them things in the mail that catch their attention. A great way to impress them is to send them a referral for their own business or give them a resource that will help them in another area of their lives.

If you want to be strategic about pulling your "Most Wanted Clients" into your business, start with a list of the top people you would jump out of bed in the morning to work with. Do a little sleuthing to find out details about them. See if you can find out about their family, hobbies, and when their birthday is. Find out what they are passionate about. Compile the information in a spreadsheet or database.

Now make a plan to reach out to them consistently. Send them things in the mail. Comment on their Facebook status. Watch for the public events they will be at and make a point of being in attendance so you can interact with them. It is all about developing a connection over time. Don't go overboard and make them feel like you are stalking them.

Interact with them like you would a friend. Not a needy, leech of a friend. Be a self-confident friend who encourages and lifts up the other person. Be more interested in finding out about them than you are in telling about yourself. Chances are they won't hire you next month, but eventually they will recognize you as someone they can trust and will look to you when they have a need that you can fill.

Developing a Most Wanted list is a great way to gradually fill your practice with juicy clients that you feel honored to work with. Make it a long term goal to develop a relationship with your most wanted clients so that when they need to hire someone, they will think of you.

© Deb Brown, Touch Your Client's Heart. Deb Brown is the founder of Touch Your Client's Heart, a client appreciation company. Touch Your Client's Heart believes the key to client retention and word of mouth referrals is as simple as client appreciation gifts, but it must be done the right way. To find out How to Make Your Clients Fall in Love With You, enter your name and email at TouchYourClientsHeart.com.

Widen your Circle - Network like an Introvert

By Soma Jurgensen

I'll admit it. I'm an extrovert and networking is generally not something that causes fear in my heart as it does for others. I'm comfortable starting conversations with people and I thrive on the activity around me. Over the last year I've learned something – when I network like an extrovert I miss out on opportunities. It's human nature that draws us to the people who are most like us, and while getting to know people like me is fun and useful, I'm missing out on a whole group of possible connections. If you've been networking the same way and feel in a rut, this article can help you widen your network.

1. Stick to the edges

As an extrovert I charge to the middle of the room and stay there. In my effort to network like an introvert I've made a commitment to start my networking at the edges. There is a different dynamic to the edges of the room where conversations haven't already started and the groups are smaller. People tend to gravitate to one or the other, the center or the edges, so you're bound to make different connections.

Benefit: Less pressure from the crowd's energy allows greater time to make connections with a smaller group of people.

2. Ask for cards selectively

The energy in the room can feel electric and cards begin flashing all around. I've learned that it's more difficult for me to make authentic connections when I'm overwhelmed by the number of cards I have to manage on the spot. Instead, I've decided to ask only for the cards of people who I believe I can help in some way. Since one of my goals is to support and give back to my network, I want to make sure to follow up with the people I meet.

Benefit: Fewer cards means you are more likely to follow up with a meaningful message.

3. Sit by yourself

This one was the hardest for me. I like to be surrounded by people so I would choose tables that were partially full at networking dinners. I've discovered the people at full tables are the same ones that gravitate to the center at events. (See tip 1) Now I sit at a table toward the edge that doesn't have anyone seated. It's a risk, but I've never sat alone. The people who join me are different; because I'm sitting alone I'm more approachable by individuals or pairs.

Benefit: Sitting alone shows you are approachable to people attending an event solo and might be intimidated by a larger group.

How will you widen your network? Use this activity to get you started.

For the next ____ networking events, I will use the
#
tip________________ so that I can get the benefit
choose from aforementioned tip
of________________.
choose from aforementioned benefit

I'll share what I learn with ______________ to make sure I
name of person
stay accountable.

© Soma D. Jurgensen, Intentional Growth Strategies. Visit IntentionalGrowthStrategies.com for resources to put your effort where you money is with clarity, focused planning, and training.

How to Turn Networking Nightmares Into Confident Connections

By Teresa Thomas

Every now and then, we experience networking gone bad. While we may cringe at the time, we can learn from these networking nightmares so we can network with confidence.

Have you ever met (or been) any of these people?

Card-happy Candice

Bio: She's handing you her business cards or brochures before you've had the chance to introduce yourself. Or she hands you several business cards (without you asking) and asks you to give her cards to everyone you know. As you leave the event, you see a bunch of her business cards in the trash (ouch for her and for the environment).

How to avoid becoming: Hold onto your business cards until you are either A) asked for one, B) expected to exchange them as part of a networking format or C) concluding your conversation and then ask the other person if they would like to exchange business cards.

Complainer Conrad

Bio: He complains about the food, the temperature, the drive, and the lack of parking to everyone he meets. He complains about the people he works with (or used to work with) or complains in general about his job. He remarks that he doesn't like someone who is at the event. He makes you wonder if he'll complain about you, too after you leave the conversation.

How to avoid becoming: If you have a complaint that needs to be heard bring your concern discreetly to the host or to someone in charge at the venue. If you do share a concern with someone you meet, do so in a way that creates conversation vs. shutting it down. For example, "The traffic coming in from the west was really heavy this morning and I was so eager to be here. How was the driving for you?"

Downer Don

Bio: He brings up all that is wrong in the world or shares only the bad things that have been happening in his life lately. He makes it so that you feel uncomfortable sharing that you enjoy your work or your latest project.

How to avoid becoming: Leave your negativity at the door and focus on being as positive as you can for the people you'll be meeting. If things are going badly for you, you can pick it back up after the event if you must. Or you might even decide to not attend the event until you are feeling in better spirits.

"It's all about me" Mimi

Bio: Everything she says or asks seems to come down to being about her. When she asks you for a coffee meeting to "learn about each other's businesses," it becomes evident that she only wants to talk about what she does. Even though she hasn't learned anything about you, she assumes that you can't be happy unless you work with her.

How to avoid becoming: Realize that you'll have a much better chance of making a great impression if you spend more time learning about the other person and less time on yourself.

By learning who the other person is and what they need, you'll be in a much better position to know what information about you they would like to hear and would find helpful.

Low-Esteem Lola

Bio: When you ask if you've met before she answers, "Oh, you would never know me. I'm only . . ." Her shoulders are slumped. When you try to talk about work, she undermines her capabilities. Since she is not confident in what she does, you realize that you would not be able to feel confident in recommending her to others.

How to avoid becoming: When you have bouts of low self-esteem, focus on what is going well. You may have to give yourself affirmations and "psych yourself up" to portray yourself at your best. When someone gives you a compliment, graciously and simply say "thank you" rather than dismissing it. Focus as much as you can on the other person and how you can help them so that you don't get so caught up in your own self-doubt. When you introduce yourself, share about what most interests you about what you do. Your eyes will then sparkle with confidence and it will be a joy for anyone who talks with you.

Long-winded Lonny

Bio: He might ask you a question but he doesn't pause for an answer. When you are talking, he constantly interjects with his own story. You run out of breath just listening to him. It's a challenge to extricate yourself from the one-sided conversation because there is never a break.

How to avoid becoming: When you ask someone a question (and be sure that you do ask questions), listen intently.

When you feel like interjecting, ask yourself first if it's really that important to share that information right now.

Demeaning Dietrich

Bio: When you introduce yourself, he makes a snide remark or jokes about your profession. Or he may inadvertently put you down by talking about someone else in your profession who is "oh-so-wonderful" thereby making it clear that he thinks you could never compare.

How to avoid becoming: Understand that when you put someone down—even in a joking way—that is what they will remember you by. Do you really want to be remembered in this way? When you focus on lifting the other person up, you lift yourself to a higher level, too.

Vague Victor

Bio: He has introduced himself and you've asked questions but you still have no clue what he does. When you ask him about his target market, he responds that he works with anyone who breathes. He uses terms like great results and satisfied customers but you don't know what the results are or who he has for customers.

How to avoid becoming: When you introduce yourself, share a specific example of how you help your clients. You don't need to worry about covering everything you offer. It will be more effective to share a brief and compelling story that leads the other person to want to know more.

Tuned-out Tony

Bio: He is more concerned about what he is going to say next than what anyone else is saying. He seems more interested in everything else going on in the room than in your conversation.

How to avoid becoming: Pay more attention to what the other person is saying and don't worry about what you will say next. The more you pay attention, the better able you will be to respond authentically and in context. While it's okay to momentarily look away, be sure that you are making regular eye contact with the people in your conversation.

Nameless Naomi

Bio: She is so interesting and you'd like to introduce her to someone else but you cannot see or read her name tag. Or, she is someone you have met before but cannot recall her name and are desperate for a clue.

How to avoid becoming: When you are at an event where people are wearing nametags, make sure you place it where people can easily read it. Be sure that your hair or clothing does not cover up the nametag. Write clearly and large enough so that other people can read it. When appropriate and at a business networking event, include your full name with your business name below. Place your nametag near your right collarbone so that it is easy for the people you meet to see it as you shake hands. Also, be sure that your nametag is not placed somewhere too embarrassing for someone else too look at it (e.g. too low on your chest or by your stomach).

Close-a-sale Claude

Bio: He is more interested in making short-term individual sales than in developing trusted relationships that lead to referrals beyond the network and repeat business. He wants to sell directly to the people he meets at events and right away.

Because of the pressure, he may indeed get some sales but those same people will avoid him next time or tell others to watch out.

How to avoid becoming: Networking is about expanding your network in a sustainable way that supports you by building trust and increasing what you would be able to accomplish on your own. A network is about creating multiple points of solid connections, like a net vs. strands of connections that easily break.

You've likely identified with at least one of the above examples – either having taken on that role yourself at times or observing it in someone else.

The aim of this article is not to make you feel badly – believe me; we all make some of these mistakes at one time or another. Rather, laugh about any setbacks you've had and use these nightmare stories to strengthen your networking skills and to steer you toward connecting with confidence.

Networking Etiquette

By Teresa Thomas

Here is a quick and easy list of networking etiquette beyond what is covered elsewhere in this book:

Appreciation:

If someone sends you a referral (even if it doesn't result in business), express your gratitude. A handwritten personalized thank you is best. At the very least, find some way to acknowledge them for their referral.

Exchanging business cards:

As a general rule, it is best to request the other person's business card before offering your own. Provide only one business card unless the other person specifically asks for more. It is more powerful for you to have their business card because then you have the information you need for taking the reins with follow up.

Exercise Restraint:

Do not ask people you have just met or who have not yet experienced your service or product to recommend your business to others. Think of it like dating and take things one step at a time. A trusted referral base takes time and experience to develop.

Along these lines, don't look at each person you meet as the direct prospect for an immediate sale. Instead, see people as unique and interesting individuals who are connected to a broad network and who may be a good fit for your own network. Most people don't attend networking events with the intention of buying something, yet too many people approach networking as a way to make a sale. Do you see the disconnect? Big picture networking is more magnetizing and will result in building business based on trust. A transactional approach to networking might result in some immediate sales but runs the risk of people avoiding you in the future or worse yet, telling others to be wary.

Follow up:

If you say you will follow up, be sure to do so. Don't make promises you can't keep. For example, if you think of the perfect resource to share with a new connection, it's better to follow up with this information as a pleasant surprise than to promise the information and then not follow through.

Greetings without a handshake:

Many people do not shake hands for a variety of reasons (e.g. cultural, religious, disability, health). If you do not shake hands, you do the person you are meeting a favor by leading the introduction in the way you wish to be greeted (e.g. a slight bow, a fist-bump, motioning the tip of a hat, raising a glass in "cheers").

If you feel as though you may be getting sick or contagious the best thing would be to stay home. When that can't be avoided, people will appreciate it if you don't spread germs through a handshake.

Handshakes:

A handshake should not distract the person you are meeting. You want them to focus on you and not how your handshake felt. A firm handshake where the hands connect at the V between the thumb and index finger sends a message of confidence. Bone-crushing, weak or finger-tips only handshakes make people feel uncomfortable.

Hugs:

Some people are huggers and others are not. It's wise to assume others are not huggers (especially when it comes to authority figures, co-workers and across gender). If you are a hugger and feel a particular affinity with the person, you can ask, "Are you a hugger?" If they say no or otherwise give the impression they are not, respect their response. If you are not a hugger, it is okay to let others know it's just not your thing without having to explain it.

Introductions:

It is customary to introduce the person with the most seniority in age, fame or position first. For example, you would introduce the featured speaker at an event first and then the guest if you are introducing them to each other.

Introducing people online:

When you introduce two people online, get permission from each of them first to make sure the introduction is welcomed. Let them know why you want to make the introduction and ask how they would like to be introduced. If they are too busy, or not interested at this time (or already know the person), it puts them into the awkward situation of determining how to respond or to risk ignoring the request. Strive to make your introductions respectful and mutually beneficial.

Meeting times:

Stay within the time you agreed to for a call or meeting. If it seems like more time would be helpful, ask if you could continue the conversation another time. For example, if you requested a short phone meeting with someone you could say, "I appreciate the information we've discussed. I want to be mindful that I had requested 20 minutes of time with you and we are nearly at 20 minutes. I would be interested in talking more. Would you be open to meeting again or could I email you a couple of other questions I have?" It's possible the other person will agree to spend a bit more time with you but this gives them a chance to gracefully complete the meeting.

Mobile devices:

Tuck your phone or other mobile device away when you are meeting with people. Don't send the message that your mobile device is more important than the people with whom you are interacting. If it's absolutely critical to take a call or check a text, excuse yourself for the inconvenience and step away to a discreet place that won't be a bother the other people.

Phone calls:

When someone is not expecting your call, be sure to ask them if the timing works for them. For example, "I'm calling about _____. Is this a good time to talk?" This allows the recipient the grace to let you know how much time they have or if another time would be better. Too often, callers launch into the reason they are calling without giving the recipient of the call a chance to interject and it can leave an annoying impression.

Social media:

When you post, consider if it is something you would be okay with having the whole world to see. Remember that on social media, the "whole world" could see it.

Know your goals for using social media. Make sure your posts fit with those goals and in ways that are engaging, interesting, informational, insightful, inspirational or otherwise useful.

Don't send connection requests to strangers with the attempt to make a sale. That's a surefire way to wreck your reputation.

Stand up:

When you are seated and are introduced to someone who is standing, it is polite to stand up and greet them at their level.

Win/Win:

Always remember that networking is a two-way street. When situations come up in networking and you are unsure of the proper etiquette, ask yourself the following simple questions:

- What feels most respectful?
- How would I want to be treated?
- What is the most mutually beneficial win/win approach?

CHAPTER NINE

Additional Resources

Brafman, Ori and Brafman, Rom. *Click: The Magic of Instant Connection.* New York: Broadway Books 2010

Cain, Susan. *Quiet: The Strength of Introverts In a World that Won't Stop Talking.* New York: Crown Publishers 2012.

Carnegie, Dale. *How to Win Friends and Influence People.* Dale Carnegie & Associates, Inc. 1936/1964/1981.

Mackay, Harvey. *Dig Your Well Before You're Thirsty: The Only Networking Book You'll Ever Need.* New York: Doubleday 1997.

Price, Ph.D, Verna Cornelia. *The Power of People: Four Kinds of People Who Can Change Your Life.* Robbinsdale, MN.: JCAMA Publishers 2002.

Rath, Tom. *Strengthfinders, 2.0.* New York: Gallup Press 2007.

Rath, Tom. *Vital Friends: The People You Can't Afford to Live Without.* New York: Gallup Press 2006.

Wagner, David. *Life as a Daymaker*. San Diego, CA: Jodere Group 2003.

Watson, MBA, Kathleen. *NetProfit: Business Networking Without the Nerves*. Andover, MN: Expert Publishing 2007.

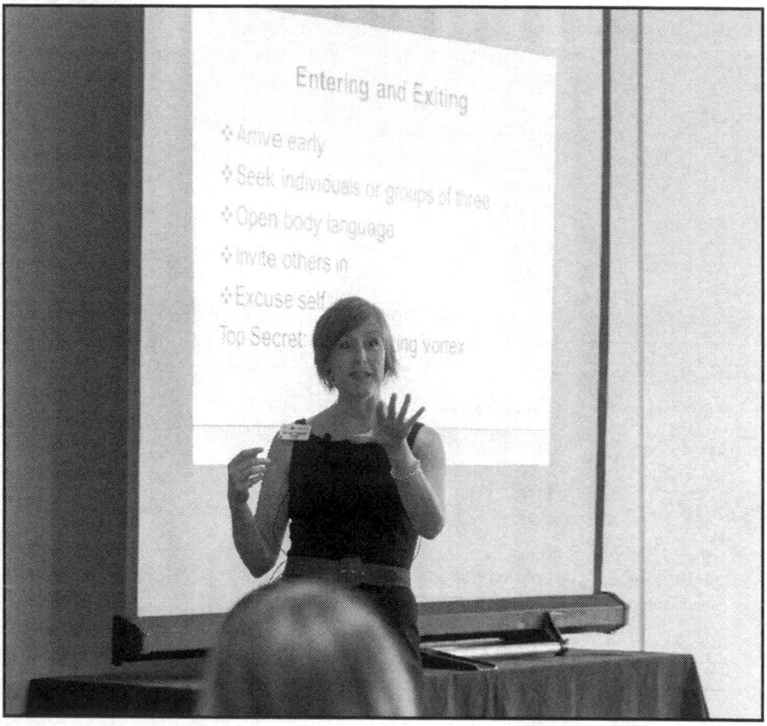

"So many 'motivational' speakers come off as intimidatingly superhuman and I feel like they encourage bluffing, posturing, and networking techniques that don't feel right for me. Teresa is none of the above! I left with concrete ideas I can use."

-Jane S. Kerr, Events Sales Manager

About the Author

Teresa Thomas believes networking is really about seeing the interconnectedness between all of us. It is about listening and noticing the ways we can lift each other up.

For over twenty years, Teresa's work has fully embraced her strengths, values and motivations to make win-win connections. In 2007, Teresa took on the leadership of WIN (MN Women In Networking) to provide quality networking events and professional development for women in business.

Are the people in your business, association, or campus ready to gain tips and techniques needed to master networking?

Teresa provides highly interactive presentations—keynotes, breakout sessions and workshops—designed to put attendees on the fast track for networking success. For groups wishing to purchase the *Win/Win Networking* connections guidebook in bulk, special pricing is available.

Please email contact@teresa-thomas.com for details.